Editor
Gisela Lee, M.A.

Editorial Manager
Karen J. Goldfluss, M.S. Ed.

Editor-in-Chief
Sharon Coan, M.S. Ed.

Cover Artist
Barb Lorseyedi

Art Coordinator
Kevin Barnes

Art Director
CJae Froshay

Imaging
Ralph Olmedo, Jr.
James Grace
Rosa C. See

Product Manager
Phil Garcia

Publisher
Mary D. Smith, M.S. Ed.

Math Games

GRADE 5

Author

Patti Sima, M.A. and Neil Jacob, M.S.

Teacher Created Resources, Inc.
6421 Industry Way
Westminster, CA 92683
www.teachercreated.com

ISBN: 978-0-7439-3725-2

©2003 Teacher Created Resources, Inc.
Reprinted, 2007
Made in U.S.A.

Table of Contents

Introduction. 3
Game 1: What's Your Sign?. 4
Game 2: Calculator Fun. 5
Game 3: More Calculator Fun. 6
Game 4: Battleship 7
Game 5: Change for a Dollar 8
Game 6: The Value of Words. 9
Game 7: Cookie Math 10
Game 8: Energy Facts 11
Game 9: Math Baseball 12
Game 10: Buzz and Bizz Buzz 13
Game 11: Cinco de Mayo Math Game 14
Game 12: Backwards Jeopardy 15
Game 13: On the Ball 17
Game 14: Time's Up 18
Game 15: Terrific Tangrams 19
Game 16: Calculated Story 21
Game 17: Take a Chance. 22
Game 18: Math Squares 23
Game 19: Roman Numerals 24
Game 20: Place Value in the News 25
Game 21: Go to Great Lengths 26
Game 22: Let's Operate. 28
Game 23: Math Card Games. 29
Game 24: Pizza Problem 30
Game 25: Riddle Math 31
Game 26: Divisibility Rules!. 32
Game 27: Volume Control! 33
Game 28: Spaceship Flip. 34
Game 29: Prime Time 36
Game 30: Factors and Multiples 37
Game 31: Decimal Derby 38
Game 32: Fractured Fractions 39
Game 33: Close the Box 40
Game 34: Magic Squares. 41
Game 35: I've Been Framed 42
Game 36: Division Mix-Up. 43
Game 37: Improper Fraction Mix-Up 44
Game 38: Parting Advice. 45
Game 39: Astounding Rounding 46

Answer Key 47

The old adage "practice makes perfect" can really hold true for your child in his or her education. The more practice and exposure your child has to concepts being taught in school, the more success he or she is likely to find. For many parents, knowing how to help your children can be frustrating because the resources may not be readily available. As a parent it is also difficult to know where to focus your efforts so that the extra practice your child receives at home supports what he or she is learning at school.

This book has been designed to help parents and teachers reinforce basic skills with their children. *Practice Makes Perfect* reviews basic math skills for children in grade 5. This book contains puzzles and games that allow children to learn, review, and reinforce basic math concepts. Games and puzzles have long proved their worth as vehicles of learning. Such activities carry with them three intrinsic powers of motivation—curiosity, competition, and delight. While it would be impossible to include all concepts taught in grade 4 in this book, the following main objectives are reinforced:

- addition
- subtraction
- multiplication
- division
- probability
- measurement and basic geometry

- locating points on a grid
- place value
- fractions
- decimals
- interpreting data
- general review

Any of the games or activities in this book may be modified to fit the needs of your group. Rules may be changed or clues may be given. Games that are designed for two players may be played on teams, or additional score sheets may be added to accommodate more players. The most important thing is for students to learn something while enjoying the game or activity.

How to Make the Most of This Book

Here are some useful ideas for optimizing the games and activities in this book:

- Set aside a specific place in your home to work on the pages. Keep it neat and tidy with materials on hand.

- Set up a certain time of day to work on the games and puzzles. This will establish consistency. An alternative is to look for times in your day or week that are less hectic and more conducive to practicing skills.

- Keep all practice sessions with your child positive and constructive. If the mood becomes tense or you and your child are frustrated, set the book aside and look for another time to practice with your child.

- Help with instructions if necessary. If your child is having difficulty understanding what to do or how to get started, work through the first steps with him or her.

- Review the work your child has done. This serves as reinforcement and provides further practice.

- Look for ways to make real-life applications to the skills being reinforced.

Game 1

What's Your Sign?

Place + or – signs between the digits so that both sides of each equation are equal.

1.	9	8	6	3	5	1	= 6
2.	5	3	4	4	2	9	= 17
3.	5	3	2	4	1	5	= 2
4.	3	2	1	4	1	3	= 6
5.	5	1	1	3	4	8	= 18
6.	4	9	3	7	3	1	= 19
7.	2	1	8	9	3	5	= 20
8.	8	7	1	4	4	6	= 14
9.	7	6	2	9	9	3	= 0
10.	3	5	3	9	6	5	= 15

Game 2

Calculator Fun

Answer each math problem with a calculator. When you have the answer, turn the calculator upside-down to find an answer for each of the clues in parentheses. The first one is done for you.

1. (Too big) $21,000 + 14,001 =$ _____ 35,001 (loose) _____

2. (A sphere) $21,553 + 16,523 =$ _____

3. (Make honey) $10,000 - 4662 =$ _____

4. (Petroleum) $142 \times 5 =$ _____

5. (Tool for watering the garden) $7008 \div 2 =$ _____

6. (Not feeling well) $348 + 424 - 1 =$ _____

7. (To cry) $0.02004 + 0.02004 =$ _____

8. (Boy's name) $9376 - 1658 =$ _____

9. (City in Idaho) $27413 + 7695 =$ _____

10. (Antonym for "tiny") $206 + 206 + 206 =$ _____

Game 3 🐚 ᧐ 🐚 ᧐ 🐚 ᧐ 🐚 ᧐ 🐚 ᧐ ᧐ 🐚 ᧐ 🐚

More Calculator Fun

Do each math problem on your calculator. Then, turn the calculator upside-down to find an answer for each of the following clues.

	Number	**Word**
1. $1,000 - 229$ = not feeling well	_____	_____
2. $5,285 + 1251 + 1199$ = the opposite of buy	_____	_____
3. $70,000 - 34,999$ = not secured	_____	_____
4. $314 + 215 + 181$ = petroleum	_____	_____
5. $0.5731 + 0.2003$ = hola	_____	_____
6. $0.09 - 0.07$ = a place for animals	_____	_____
7. $188,308 + 188,308$ = to laugh in a silly way	_____	_____
8. $2,000 + 95 + 700 + 250$ = foot apparel	_____	_____
9. $1080 - 272$ = Robert's nickname	_____	_____
10. $0.20202 + 0.20202$ = Santa's laughter	_____	_____
11. $926 \times 2 \times 2$ = an empty space	_____	_____
12. $3544 + 3011 + 550$ = synonym for dirt	_____	_____
13. $801 - 163$ = to ask earnestly	_____	_____
14. 101×5 = a call for help	_____	_____
15. $.3 \times .3$ = the opposite of stop	_____	_____

Game 4 ❧ ❧ ❧ ❧ ❧ ❧ ❧ ❧ ❧ ❧ ❧ ❧ ❧

Battleship

Equipment: paper and pencil for each team or player (Graph paper can be used but is not necessary.)

Directions

- The object of the game is to sink your opponent's battleship by making the right "hits" on a grid.

- Before beginning play, two naval battlefields per player need to be drawn. Each player should draw a grid of 10 blocks down and 10 blocks across for a total of 100 blocks. The blocks don't need to be very big. A quarter of an inch is large enough.

- The blocks should be numbered 1 through 10 along the top row of the grid. Letter the blocks A through J along the left edge of the grids. One grid should be labeled for the player, and the other should be labeled for the enemy.

- Players then must place battleships on the grid for their respective "sides" by drawing lines through consecutive blocks to indicate their ships' positions. Each player has four ships: an aircraft carrier of four blocks, a cruiser of three blocks, and two destroyers of two blocks apiece.

- The battleships are marked on the grids without letting the opponent see the positions. The blocks must be located on a straight line—horizontally, vertically, or diagonally. A battleship may not be split up.

- When the grids are drawn and the battleships are in place, the players should determine who fires first. Whoever begins gets 11 shots to hit the other player's battleships.

- The player calls out blocks of the grid according to letter and number: C-9, G-8, and so on, until he or she has used up 11 shots. As the shots are being fired, the defensive player should mark them on his or her own grid with a number 1. This represents the first round. The firing player should also keep track of where his or her shots were fired by marking 1 on his or her second grid for the enemy.

- After all 11 shots have been fired, the defensive player calls out each shot and announces whether or not it was a hit. It's a hit if it is on one of the squares marked for the battleship. It is a miss if it is on an empty square. Players should circle the squares that represent a hit to distinguish them from a miss.

- The process is repeated for the second player.

- During the second round, each player gets 11 shots minus the hits he or she scored in the first round. If a player made four hits, then he or she is allowed only seven shots in the second round. The number two indicates the second round.

- The object of the game is to sink battleships, so shots should be called in the vicinity of previous hits. Once all of the blocks constituting a ship have been hit, the battleship is sunk.

- The game is over once all of a player's battleships have been sunk. Each player must announce when his or her battleship is sunk.

Game 5 ☙ ☙ ☙ ☙ ☙ ☙ ☙ ☙ ☙ ☙ ☙ ☙ ☙

Change for a Dollar

There are over 200 ways to make change for a dollar. Work with a friend to list as many ways as you can. List the coins in order on each line, from largest to smallest. (**Hint:** Working from large to small coins will help you find more ways to make change, too.) The list has been started for you. If you need more space, continue your list on the back of this paper.

Use the following abbreviations:

hd *(half dollar)*   **q** *(quarter)*   **d** *(dime)*   **n** *(nickel)*   **p** *(penny)*

1. 2hd		26.
2. 1hd and 2q		27.
3. 1hd and 5d		28.
4. 1hd and 10n		29.
5.		30.
6.		31.
7.		32.
8.		33.
9.		34.
10.		35.
11.		36.
12.		37.
13.		38.
14.		39.
15.		40.
16.		41.
17.		42.
18.		43.
19.		44.
20.		45.
21.		46.
22.		47.
23.		48.
24.		49.
25.		50.

Game 6 ༄ ༂ ༄ ༂ ༄ ༂ ༄ ༂ ༄ ༂ ༄ ༂ ༄

The Value of Words

In the value box, each letter of the alphabet has been given a dollar value. To find the value of a word, add the values of all the letters. For example, the word "school" would be worth $72 (19 + 3 + 8 + 15 + 15 + 12 = 72). Write words with appropriate values in each of the boxes below.

$10–$20 Words	$21–$50 Words
$51–$75 Words	**$76–$100 Words**
$101–$150 Words	**$151–$200 Words**

VALUE BOX	
A =	$1
B =	$2
C =	$3
D =	$4
E =	$5
F =	$6
G =	$7
H =	$8
I =	$9
J =	$10
K =	$11
L =	$12
M =	$13
N =	$14
O =	$15
P =	$16
Q =	$17
R =	$18
S =	$19
T =	$20
U =	$21
V =	$22
W =	$23
X =	$24
Y =	$25
Z =	$26

Game 7 ❧ ə ❧ ə ❧ ə ❧ ə ❧ ə ə ❧ ❧

Cookie Math

The following word problems are based on some interesting statistics about chocolate chip cookies.

> **Fact A:** *Seven billion chocolate chip cookies are consumed annually in the United States.*

Exercises

1. Write seven billion in numerals. _____

2. In order to find out how many cookies are consumed on average by every person in the United States, what other information would you need to know in order to solve the problem? _____

3. Where could you find that information? _____

4. How would you solve the problem? _____

> **Fact B:** *Ninety million bags of chocolate morsels are sold each year, enough to make 150 million pounds (67.5 kg) of cookies.*

Exercises

1. Write a ratio to show the number of bags of chocolate morsels to the number of pounds of cookies. _____

   Reduce it to its lowest terms. _____

2. How many pounds of cookies can be made from 30 million bags of chocolate morsels? How could this problem be solved? _____

> **Fact C:** *The 150 million pounds (67.5 million kg) of cookies in fact number 2 above is enough to circle the globe 10 times.*

Exercises

1. How many cookies does it take to circle the globe once? _____

2. How many cookies would it take to circle the globe 15 times? _____

> **Fact D:** *Although the original Toll House burned to the ground in 1984, it was still baking cookies in an annex until the new one was rebuilt. Some thirty-three thousand cookies a day were baked there.*

Exercises

1. If 33,000 cookies were baked there each day, how many cookies will be baked in a week? _____

2. If baking goes on 24 hours a day, how many cookies, on the average, are baked each hour? _____

Game 8 ꙮ ꙮ ꙮ ꙮ ꙮ ꙮ ꙮ ꙮ ꙮ ꙮ ꙮ ꙮ ꙮ

Energy Facts

Directions: Learn some interesting facts about energy as you solve the problems below. Then write the letters from the box on the sentence blanks, matching the letters with the corresponding answers below the blanks.

A	C	D	E	G	H
37 x 12 = ____	659 + 13 = ____	720 ÷ 16 = ____	316 – 105 = ____	67 + 39 = ____	374 ÷ 22 = ____
I	**K**	**L**	**M**	**N**	**O**
823 – 78 = ____	16 X 15 = ____	361 + 19 = ____	957 ÷ 33 = ____	500 – 135 = ____	17 X 9 = ____
R	**S**	**T**	**U**	**W**	**Y**
369 + 72 = ____	216 ÷ 8 = ____	999 –955 = ____	62 X 4 = ____	416 + 41 = ____	488 ÷ 4 = ____

Energy Facts

1. Anything that moves has energy of ____ ____ ____ ____ ____ ____.

29   153   44   745   153   365

2. Energy of motion is called ____ ____ ____ ____ ____ ____ ____ energy.

240   745   365   211   44   745   672

3. ____ ____ ____ ____ and waterfalls have kinetic energy.

457   745   365   45

4. All light is ____ ____ ____ ____ ____ ____.

211   365   211   441   106   122

5. ____ ____ ____ ____ is energy.

17   211   444   44

6. ____ ____ ____ ____ ____ is energy.

27   153   248   365   45

7. ____ ____ ____ ____ ____ ____ ____ ____ ____ ____ ____ is energy.

211   380   211   672   44   441   745   672   745   44   122

8. One kind of energy can be ____ ____ ____ ____ ____ ____ ____ to another kind of energy.

672   17   444   365   106   211   45

Game 9

Math Baseball

Directions

- The object of the game is to score runs by correctly answering multiplication problems which will advance runners around the bases.

- Up to 10 children can play at a time.

- Create a small playing field by placing four bases in the shape of a baseball field diamond about six to eight feet (two to three meters) apart.

- The players should be divided into two equal teams. One team represents the "field" as the pitcher, catcher, and first, second, and third basemen. The other team is the batting team.

- The batter steps up to home plate, and the pitcher calls out a multiplication problem. The problem should be appropriate to the skill and age level of the players. One example could be five times three. The catcher and batter should respond as quickly as they can. If the batter answers first, then he or she advances to first base. If the catcher answers first, then the batter is out.

- The next player who comes to bat is given a problem and either advances or is put out. If the batter answers correctly, then any other players on base get to advance.

- The pitcher can try to put runners out by calling out problems to them. If the baseman answers correctly, then the runner is out. If the runner answers correctly, then he gets to advance by stealing a base.

- The teams switch places after three outs. The players can change positions from inning to inning so that others get a chance to be the pitcher or catcher.

- The team with the most runs at the end of nine innings wins the game. The game can be played with a fewer number of innings, of course.

Game 10

Buzz and Bizz Buzz

Directions for Buzz

- The object of this game is to count to 100, all the while substituting the word "buzz" for the number seven or any multiple of seven.

- Players line up and take turns counting, each player saying one number at a time. For example, players would count to 20 as follows:

  1, 2, 3, 4, 5, 6, BUZZ, 8, 9, 10, 11, 12, 13, BUZZ, 15, 16, BUZZ (because 17 has a 7 in it), 18, 19, 20.

- When a player misses, the group must start counting at 1 again.

Directions for Bizz Buzz

- This game is played just like Buzz (see above), but in addition to the sevens or any multiple of seven being replaced with the word "buzz", fives or multiples of five are replaced with the word "bizz."

- For example, counting from 25 to 40 would be as follows:

  BIZZ, 26, BUZZ, BUZZ, 29, BIZZ, 31, 32, 33, 34, BIZZ-BUZZ (because 35 is a multiple of 5 and 7), 36, BUZZ, 38, 39, BIZZ.

Game 11 ෳ ෴ ෳ ෴ ෳ ෴ ෳ ෴ ෳ ෳ ෳ ෴ ෳ ෴

Cinco de Mayo Math Game

Equipment: blackboard or paper for directions to be displayed, paper, and pencil

Directions

- Any number of players is possible.
- Using the numbers listed below, answer the questions that follow.

> ### 27, 19, 2, 129, 9, 48

1. Multiply the largest number by the smallest.

   _____

2. Triple the answer for number 1.

   _____

3. Find the average of the six numbers. Add it to number 2.

   _____

4. Find the difference between the two largest numbers. Subtract it from number 3.

   _____

5. Double number 4.

   _____

6. Multiply number 5 by the second smallest number.

   _____

7. Double the smallest number and then divide it into number 6.

   _____

8. Multiply the third largest number by the fourth largest number. Subtract the product from number 7.

   _____

9. Multiple the largest number by 10. Subtract this product from number 8.

   _____

10. Multiply the third smallest number by 20. Add the product to number 9. Subtract the second smallest number from that sum.

    _____

The year that Cinco de Mayo became important was _____, the number revealed by the correct answer to number 10.

Game 12 ⟳ ⟲ ⟳ ⟲ ⟳ ⟲ ⟳ ⟲ ⟳ ⟲ ⟳ ⟲ ⟳ ⟲

Backwards Jeopardy

Equipment: copy of the questions (page 16), scissors, paper plates or sturdy construction paper, tape, chalk, marker, blackboard, and paste

Game Preparation

1. Cut out questions (page 16) and tape one question to the back of each paper plate.

2. Write proper point amounts on the front of each plate. Write category headings in chalk on the blackboard and tape the plates according to point amounts under each heading. (See chart below.)

Directions

- The children should be divided up into two or three groups. Provide enough scratch paper for each child.

- The children determine the order in which they will take turns and have them sit in that order.

- The game begins with the turn-taker choosing a category and point amount.

- One member of a group lifts a plate and reads the question aloud. The children may work the problem or choose to pass to the opposing team. If the question is answered correctly, the teacher will remove the plate and give it to the correct team. When all the paper plates are gone, each team will add up its points to determine the winner.

Backwards Jeopardy

Fractions	Measurements	Word Problems	Time
10			
100			
1,000			
10,000			
100,000			

Game 12 *(cont.)*

Backwards Jeopardy *(cont.)*

Fractions		Measurement		Word Problems		Time	
10	10	10	10	10	10	10	10
Give two equivalent fractions for $\frac{1}{2}$.		How many inches are in one foot?		Add or Subtract? Sammie sold 87 ears of corn and 115 apples. How many more apples than ears of corn did she sell?		Give another name for 2:45 P.M.	
100	100	100	100	100	100	100	100
Simplify 3/15.		Complete: 6 yards = _____ feet.		35 students are studying Spanish, and three times that many are studying French. How many are studying French?		Three hours = _____ minutes	
1,000	1,000	1,000	1,000	1,000	1,000	1,000	1,000
Turn $\frac{8}{3}$ into a mixed number.		3 quarts + _____ quart = one gallon.		Food at summer camp costs $4.75 per camper per day. How much will it cost to feed all 12 campers for one week?		240 minutes = _____ hours.	
10,000	10,000	10,000	10,000	10,000	10,000	10,000	10,000
Add the following: $1\frac{1}{3} + 4\frac{1}{2} + 2\frac{1}{3}$		What are the two units of measurement used to measure temperature?		What is the extra information? Toni studied science for $\frac{3}{4}$ hour and then roller-bladed for one hour before dinner. After dinner she studied $1\frac{1}{2}$ more hours. How long did she study altogether?		Four days and four hours = _____ hours.	
100,000	100,000	100,000	100,000	100,000	100,000	100,000	100,000
Don was 68 $\frac{1}{8}$" tall last year. Now he is 69 $\frac{1}{2}$" tall. How much has he grown?		What is the formula used to find the area of a triangle?		What is the extra information? Apples sell for $3.50 per 10-pound bag. Cassie picked apples for 6 hours. How much money did she make?		How much time has gone by from 8:10 A.M. to 12:15 P.M.?	

Game 13

On the Ball

Directions

Have the students sit in a circle. One student starts the activity by rolling the ball to another student and saying a number between one and five. Each additional student who receives the ball will either say an additional number or the answer to the problem, according to the pattern below.

First Player: Says a number from one to five and rolls the ball to another player.

Group: Says "*Plus.*"

Second Player: Says a number from one to five and rolls the ball to another player.

Group: Says "*Equals.*"

Third Player: Says the sum of the first two numbers, repeats the sum, and rolls the ball to another player.

Group: Says "*Plus.*"

Fourth Player: Says a number from one to five and rolls the ball to another player.

Group: Says "*Equals.*"

Fifth Player: Says the sum of the two numbers, repeats the sum, and rolls the ball to another player.

This continues until the number reaches 100 or any other predetermined number.

Variations

This game may be played using more advanced operations or with larger numbers. For example, the first player would say "*three,*" and roll the ball. The second player might say "*times*" and roll the ball to the third player who might say "*six.*" Any time a complete equation is said, the whole group must say "*equals,*" so that the fourth player would say "*eighteen*" and then pass it to another player, who could either say "*plus,* "*times,*" "*minus,*" or "*divided by.*" This game may be played to eliminate students who answer incorrectly or for a predetermined amount of time.

Game 14

Time's Up

In random order, place the numbers 1 to 100 around the classroom. The students will have 10 seconds to find and touch the correct answer to the math question which you have read. This can be played as a team activity or with the whole class playing at once. If playing in teams, team members take turns being the representative for their team. You may wish to award points only to the first player who touches the correct answer.

1. What is 3 times 7?

2. How many hours are in 420 minutes?

3. What is 81 divided by 9?

4. What is the remainder in the problem 37 divided by 5?

5. What is 56 divided by 7?

6. What is the square root of 49?

7. How many feet are in 60 inches?

8. What is 9 times 2?

9. What is 14 plus 45 plus 10?

10. What is 150 minus 58?

11. How many eggs are in three dozen?

12. What is 5 squared?

13. What is 96 minus 43?

14. What is 24 plus 67?

15. How many ounces are in two pounds?

16. What is 32 divided by 4?

17. What is the remainder of 67 divided by 8?

18. How many pints are in a gallon?

19. How many quarts are in five gallons?

20. What is 48 plus 37?

Game 15

Terrific Tangrams

Equipment: a tangram pattern (page 20) and scissors

Directions

Cut out the tangram pattern on page 20. Cut the shapes apart. Experiment with the shapes. Make the tangrams into shapes as illustrated below. Next, create animals of their own, using all seven tangram pieces. Make other objects such as houses, cars, shapes, or letters of the alphabet. Compare the different ways the same objects were made.

Variation

Create an object and trace around the edge of the picture. Exchange the outlines and see if another person can recreate the tangram pattern.

Game 15 *(cont.)*

Terrific Tangrams *(cont.)*

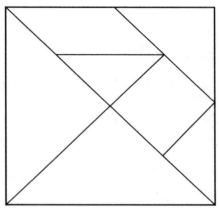

**small tangram
puzzle pattern**

large tangram puzzle pattern

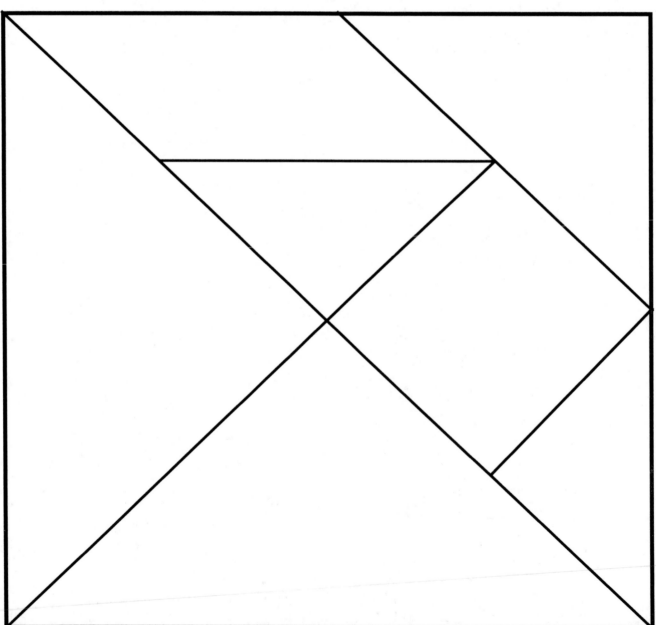

Game 16 ∂ ☙ ∂ ☙ ∂ ☙ ∂ ☙ ∂ ∂ ☙ ∂ ☙

Calculated Story

To complete this story, solve the math problems on a calculator and then turn the calculator upside down to read the word. Write the word in the blank.

Once upon a time, a girl named _____ broke her _____ when she
(45,678 − 14,105)   (123 + 814)

fell down a _____. Her friend _____ came over to say
(38,570 ÷ 5)   (9 x 33 + 40)

"_____." _____ brought _____ an
(2 + 2 + 10)   (9 x 33 + 40)   (45,678 − 14,105)

_____. But when _____ saw _____ quickly
(2979 ÷ 3)   (9 x 33 + 40)   (45,678 − 14,105)

_____ it down, she broke into
(300,000 + 70,000 + 8,800 + 9)

_____. _____ told _____,
(5 x 1,000,000 + 379,919)   (9 x 33 + 40)   (45,678 − 14,105)

"_____! You're not supposed to eat the _____!"
(9 x 501)   (386,725 ÷ 5)

Now, try to find some new calculator words.

Number	**Word**
_____	_____
_____	_____
_____	_____
_____	_____
_____	_____
_____	_____
_____	_____

Game 17

Take a Chance

Equipment: score sheet below, die, pen or pencil, and play coins

This game requires strategy and is a good review for counting money. Be sure all the children understand the directions before playing in small groups. Explain that high numbers rolled should be used in half-dollar and quarter columns because those are worth more money, and low numbers should be used with lower money amounts.

Directions

Player one rolls the die and enters the number rolled in the column under one of the coin amounts that he or she has chosen. He or she then receives that number of the coins chosen. It then becomes the next player's turn. Play continues until all players have had five turns. A player may not change his or her mind after a turn is over. Players add up their money, and whoever has the most money is the winner.

	Half-Dollar	Quarter	Dime	Nickel	Penny
Player 1					
Player 2					
Player 3					
Player 4					
Player 5					

Game 18

Math Squares

Cut out the boxes below. Arrange them so that each touching edge has the same answer.

21 33 9 x 5	**2 x 22** 76 — 16 x 2	**5 x 5** 60 ÷ 5 4 x 8	**45** 4 x 19
3 x 4 16 — 3 x 5 4 x 8	**32** 49 ÷ 7 — 42 12	**15** 9 x 9 — 4 x 16	**3 x 11** 44 — 6 x 10 7
7 x 9 64	**4 x 5** 7 x 8 3 x 6	**28** 5 x 12 — 96 4 x 4	2 x 10 — 63 2 x 6
54 7 x 4 3 x 7	9 x 6 18	**6 x 7** 36 ÷ 2 — 4 x 9	**3 x 6** 50 ÷ 2

Game 19 ᴅ ᴄ ᴅ ᴄ ᴅ ᴄ ᴅ ᴄ ᴅ ᴄ ᴅ ᴄ ᴅ ᴄ ᴅ ᴄ

Roman Numerals

Roman numerals were used many years ago to name numbers. Roman numerals can still be found today on clocks, in books to name chapters, and in books and other publications to name copyright dates. Roman numerals use capital letters to name numbers. The Roman numeral system is not a place-value system; instead, it is based on addition and subtraction. Each symbol may not be repeated more than three times.

The basic numerals are as follows:

I = 1	X = 10	C = 100	M = 1,000
V = 5	L = 50	D = 500	

Here are some more examples.

1. I	13. XIII	60. LX
2. II	14. XIV (ten plus one-before-five)	70. LXX
3. III	19. XIX	80. LXXX
4. IV (five before one)	20. XX	90. XC
5. V	29. XXIX	100. C
6. VI (one plus five)	30. XXX	200. CC
7. VII	34. XXXIV	300. CCC
8. VIII (three more than five)	39. XXXIX	400. CD
9. IX	40. XL	500. D
10. X	44. XLIV	600. DC
11. XI	49. XLIX	900. CM
12. XII	50. L	1,000. M

Write each Roman numeral in standard form.

1. XV _____

2. XXXVIII _____

3. XLIV _____

4. LXIX _____

5. LXXV _____

6. XCI _____

7. XCIX _____

8. XCV _____

9. CXVII _____

10. CXLI _____

Write each standard number in Roman numerals.

11. 409 _____

12. 1,115 _____

13. 1,661 _____

14. 1,750 _____

15. 1,940 _____

16. 12 _____

17. 14 _____

18. 29 _____

19. 1,824 _____

20. 1,949 _____

Game 20 ꙮ ꙮ ꙮ ꙮ ꙮ ꙮ ꙮ ꙮ ꙮ ꙮ ꙮ ꙮ ꙮ ꙮ

Place Value in the News

Numbers are found and used in many ways in our daily lives. Use the samples below to answer the questions and then use a newspaper to find at least 10 numbers with four or more digits, either whole numbers or decimals. Then make up 10 of your own questions and exchange with a partner.

EXTRA!!! 𝕿𝖍𝖊 𝕿𝖎𝖒𝖊𝖘 EXTRA!!!

- 52,123 People Watch the Bulls Win

- $2,196 Raised from Cookie Sale

- 17,184 students enrolled at the university.

- 4,350 Miles Ridden on a Bicycle!

- The population of the city is 673,801.

- The trip will cost $8,912.

- There are 3,007 members worldwide.

- Smith won by 2,399 votes.

- There are 7,016 acres for sale.

- 28,355 cases of the flu were reported this year.

1. What is the sum of all the four-digit numbers?_____

2. What is the sum of all the numbers that have an 8 in the thousands place?_____

3. What is the sum of all the numbers with a 1 in the hundreds place? _____

4. What is the difference between the greatest and the least numbers? _____

5. Find the sum of all the numbers that are 28,000 or greater. _____

6. What is the sum of all the numbers with an even number in the ones place? _____

7. Find the difference between the two greatest numbers. _____

8. Find the sum of all the numbers that are dollar amounts._____

9. List all the numbers that have a number greater than four in the hundreds place. _____

Game 21

Go to Great Lengths

Divide the children into teams of four. Copy and hand out a set of the task cards below to each team. The first team to successfully answer all the questions is the winner.

Task Cards

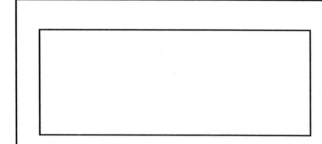

1. Rectangle

- Length = 13 feet

- Perimeter = 42 feet

- Width = _____ feet

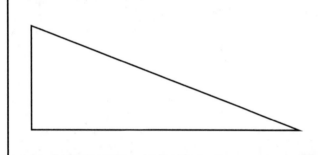

2. Triangle

- Side 1 = 29 centimeters

- Side 2 = 23 centimeters

- Perimeter = 86 centimeters

- Side 3 = _____ centimeters

3. Square

- Length of each side = 31 centimeters

- Area = _____ cm²

4. Rectangle

- Length = 18 meters

- Area = 162 meters squared

- Width = _____ meters

Game 21 *(cont.)*

Go to Great Lengths *(cont.)*

Task Cards

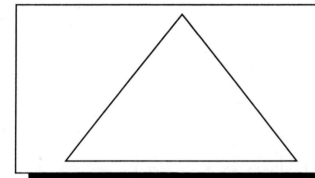

5. **Triangle**
   - Side 1 = 18 inches
   - Sides 2 and 3 are equal.
   - Perimeter = 42 inches
   - Side 2 = _____ inches
   - Side 3 = _____ inches

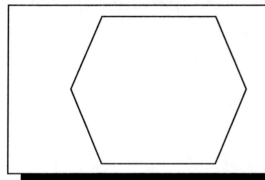

6. **Hexagon**
   - All sides are 17 feet.
   - Perimeter = _____ feet

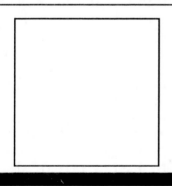

7. **Square**
   - Area = 49 square meters
   - Length of each side = _____ meters

8. **Rectangle**
   - Width = 9 feet
   - Length = 18 feet
   - Area = _____ feet^2

Game 22 ∂ ☙ ∂ ☙ ∂ ☙ ∂ ☙ ∂ ☙ ∂ ∂ ☙ ☙ ☙

Let's Operate

You will need a deck of cards for each group of four people playing the game. Cut the deck. Whoever gets the high card goes first and then play continues in a clockwise direction. The object of the game is to use addition, subtraction, multiplication, or division to cross out all the numbers from one to twenty on the score sheet. The first player flips up three cards and must use those numbers in any combination of operations to equal one of the numbers. Aces are worth one point, and face cards are worth ten points. For example, if a person turns over a king, a four, and a seven, there are many different options. Ten plus four minus seven equals seven, so the seven could be checked off; or ten minus four equals six plus seven equals thirteen, so the thirteen may be crossed off. The first person to check off all the numbers is the winner. Be sure to model the game so that people understand how to play it.

	1	2	3	4	5	6	7	8	9	10	11	12	13	14	15	16	17	18	19	20
Player 1																				
Player 2																				
Player 3																				
Player 4																				

Game 23

Math Card Games

Multiplication War

This is a game for two players, and it is played like the card game War. But instead of the player with the highest card taking the cards, the first player to correctly call out the *product of the two cards* takes them. In this game aces count as one, and face cards count as ten. To play the game, deal out the whole deck between two players. At the same time, each player flips over the top card, and the first player to correctly say the product wins both cards and puts them on the bottom of his or her deck. For example, if one player flips over a king and the other player flips over a five, the first person to say "fifty" wins both cards. The player who ends up with the whole deck is the winner; or you may play for a predetermined amount of time, and whoever has the most cards wins.

Division Destiny

This game requires a deck of playing cards. Players may use calculators or do the math with pencil and paper. Players may cut the deck to see who goes first. The first player draws three cards from the deck and multiplies them. He or she then draws a fourth card and divides the product by this number. The number is then recorded.

You may decide to use remainders or decimals or simply round to the nearest whole number. After each player has had three turns, the scores are totaled. The player with the highest number is the winner.

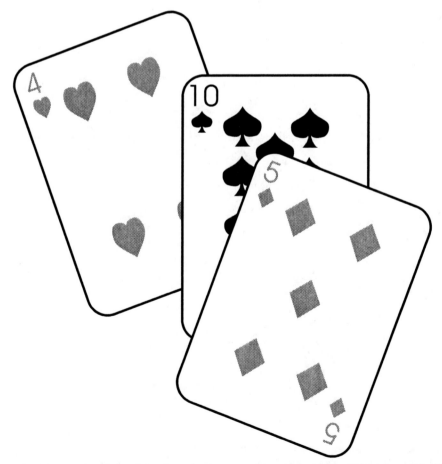

Game 24 ꙮ

Pizza Problem

The Pronto Pizza store has just sorted its pizza into several special display boxes. By looking at the boxes, you can tell where to find specific types of pizza.

- The triangle tray has pizza with pepperoni.
- The round tray has pizza with sausage.
- The rectangular tray has pizza with onions.

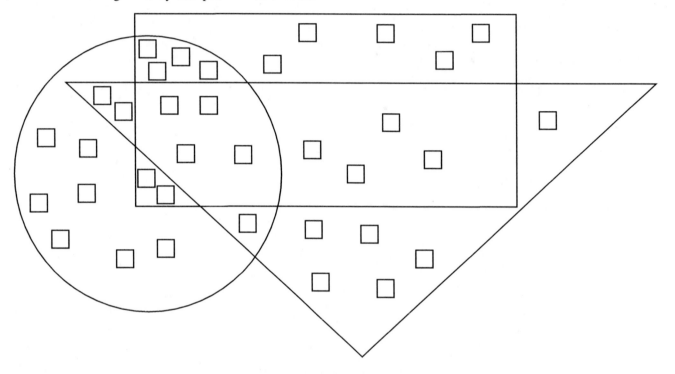

Study the boxes and their sections. Read the statement below and write your answers on the lines provided.

Find how many slices of pizza have the following:

1. only pepperoni _____

2. only sausage _____

3. only onions _____

4. pepperoni and sausage but no onions _____

5. sausage and onions but no pepperoni _____

6. onions and pepperoni but no sausage _____

7. no onions _____

8. no pepperoni _____

9. no sausage _____

10. all three ingredients—sausage, pepperoni, and onions—together _____

Game 25 ꙮ ꙮ ꙮ ꙮ ꙮ ꙮ ꙮ ꙮ ꙮ ꙮ ꙮ ꙮ

Riddle Math

How Do You Make a Hot Dog Stand?

The answer to this riddle is written in a special code at the bottom of this page. Each pair of numbers stands for a point on the graph. Write the letter shown at the point near the intersection of each pair of numbers. Read numbers across and then up. The letters will spell out the answer to the riddle.

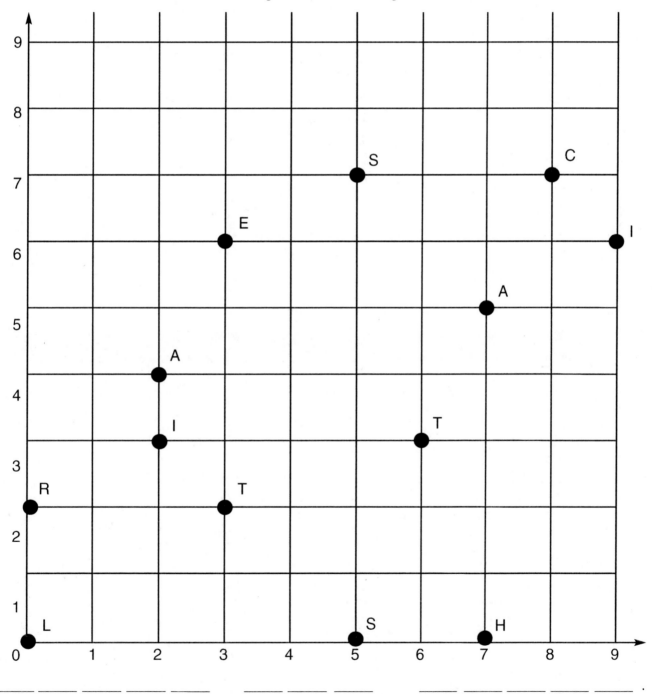

___ ___ ___ ___ ___   ___ ___ ___   ___ ___ ___ ___ ___ .
(5, 7) (6, 3) (3, 6) (7, 5) (0, 0)   (2, 3) (3, 2) (5, 0)   (8, 7) (7, 0) (2, 4) (9, 6) (0, 2)

Game 26

Divisibility Rules!

You probably already know that any even number is divisible by 2 and that any two-or-more-digit number ending in 0 is divisible by 10. But did you know there are simple ways to discover if a number is divisible by 3, 4, 5, and 9? Read the rules below and then complete the table by putting a check mark under each number that applies.

Rules

2 A number is divisible by 2 if it ends in 0, 2, 4, 6, or 8.
Example: 356 is divisible by 2 because the number in the ones place is 6.

3 A number is divisible by 3 if the sum of the digits is divisible by 3.
Example: 516 is divisible by 3 because 5 plus 1 plus 6 equals 12, and 12 is divisible by 3.

4 A number is divisible by 4 if the last two digits form a number that is divisible by 4.
Example: 3,532 is divisible by 4 because 32 is divisible by 4.

5 A number is divisible by 5 if the ones digit is 5 or 0.
Example: 670 is divisible by 5 because the ones digit is 0.

9 A number is divisible by 9 if the sum of the digits is divisible by 9.
Example: 270 is divisible by 9 because 2 plus 7 plus 0 is 9, and 9 is divisible by 9.

10 A number is divisible by 10 if the ones digit is 0.
Example: 3,400 is divisible by 10 because there is a 0 in the ones place.

Complete the table below. The check marks in the example show that 3,285 is divisible by 3, 5, and 9.

	Number	Divisible By					
		2	3	4	5	9	10
Example	3,285		✓		✓	✓	
1.	57						
2.	310						
3.	108						
4.	4,325						
5.	232						
6.	135						
7.	3,870						
8.	3,720						
9.	18,411						
10.	891						

Game 27

Volume Control!

To find the volume of a rectangular prism, multiply the length times the width times the height (or l x w x h). Since a cube has equal sides, to find the volume of a cube, simply multiply the length times the width times the height (or side x side x side since all sides are of equal length). Don't forget that volume is represented in cubic units.

(1)   **Rectangular Prism**

Volume = 120 cu. in.

Length = 5 in.

Height = 3 in.

Width = _____

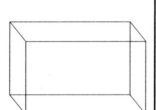

(5)   **Cube**

Length of Side = 7 in.

Volume = _____

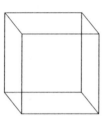

(2) Volume = 336 cm³

Height = 8 cm

Width = 6 cm

Length = _____

(6) Volume = 125 cm³

Length of Side =

_____

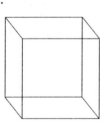

(3) Length = 11 cm

Height = 10 cm

Width = 11 cm

Volume = _____

(7) Length of Side = 10 in.

Volume = _____

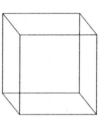

(4) Volume = 24 cu. in.

Height = 3 in.

Width = 4 in.

Length = _____

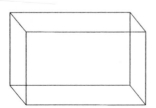

(8) Volume = 8 cm³

Length of Side =

_____

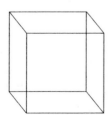

Game 28

Spaceship Flip

This game will help you better understand some basic geometry concepts. Anyone who is a fan of the video game *Tetris* will enjoy this game. The object of the game is to color more of the spaceship than your opponent does. You and a friend can work in groups of two. Each player should have a copy of the spaceship on page 35, a set of the shapes below cut out, and a crayon or marker to color the squares.

To prepare for the game, players should make a spinner by placing a pencil or pen with a paper clip around it in the middle of the circle below.

The first player spins the spinner to determine which shape to color on his or her spaceship. Players may use the cutout shapes to help them visualize how the shape would look if turned or flipped. Once a player determines which squares of the spaceship to choose, he or she should color in those squares. The next player repeats the process. If a player spins on a shape that he or she cannot fill in, then he or she is out. The game is over when both players are out. The player who colors more of the spaceship is the winner.

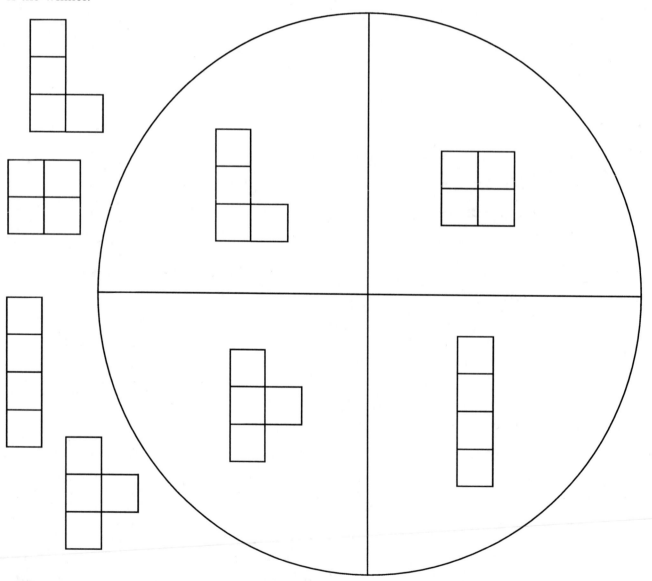

Game 28 (cont.)

Spaceship Flip (cont.)

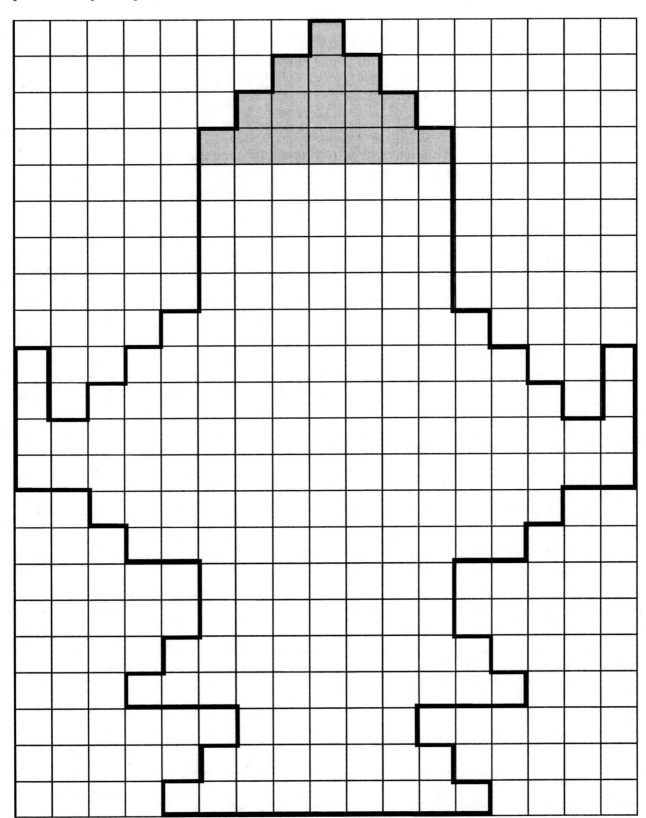

Game 29

Prime Time

Mathematicians put numbers into two categories—*prime* or *composite*. A prime number is a number with only two factors: one and itself. A composite number has more than two factors.

A Greek mathematician named Eratosthenes invented a method to see if a number is prime or composite; that method is called the *Sieve of Eratosthenes*. He arranged the numbers from 1 to 100 and used divisibility rules to find the prime numbers. Use the numbers in the box below and follow the steps to find the prime numbers.

- The number 1 is a special case. It is neither prime nor composite. Put a box around number 1.
- Number 2 is a prime number, so circle 2. Cross out all the numbers divisible by 2.
- Number 3 is a prime number, so circle 3. Then cross out all numbers divisible by 3.
- The next uncrossed number is 5. Circle 5 and then cross off all the multiples of 5.
- Circle 7. 7 is a prime number. Cross off all the multiples of 7.
- Any numbers that are left are prime, so circle them.

1	2	3	4	5	6	7	8	9	10
11	12	13	14	15	16	17	18	19	20
21	22	23	24	25	26	27	28	29	30
31	32	33	34	35	36	37	38	39	40
41	42	43	44	45	46	47	48	49	50
51	52	53	54	55	56	57	58	59	60
61	62	63	64	65	66	67	68	69	70
71	72	73	74	75	76	77	78	79	80
81	82	83	84	85	86	87	88	89	90
91	92	93	94	95	96	97	98	99	100

Game 30

Factors and Multiples

This is a game for two players. Using the numbers below, the first player marks a O on a multiple—for example, 15. The next player marks an X on each of the factors of that multiple. In this example, the second player would mark an X on 1, 3, 5, and 15.

Then, the second player marks a new multiple with X, and the first player marks O's on all the unmarked multiples of that number. A player may not mark a number that is marked already.

A player may only mark a multiple that still has some factors remaining for the opponent to mark.

When there are no multiples left that have factors to mark, the game is over. Total the number of X's and O's. The player with the most numbers marked is the winner.

1	2	3	4	5
6	7	8	9	10
11	12	13	14	15
16	17	18	19	20
21	22	23	24	25
26	27	28	29	30

Game 31 ⋰ ⋰ ⋰ ⋰ ⋰ ⋰ ⋰ ⋰ ⋰ ⋰ ⋰ ⋰

Decimal Derby

This is a game for two players. The object of the game is to make two numbers and find their product. Whoever has the greater number is the winner.

Use index cards or regular playing cards to make the numbers 0 through 9. If using playing cards, have a face card represent 0 and the ace represent 1.

Shuffle the cards and place them facedown. Player one draws the top card and writes the number somewhere on his or her sheet. Then player two repeats the process. This continues until both players have drawn four cards and written the numbers on their game sheets. Once a number has been written on the sheet, it cannot be changed. Both players should then find the products of both numbers. If they disagree about the product, a calculator may be used to determine the correct answer. The player with the greater product is the winner.

Player One Game Sheet

Player Two Game Sheet

Game 32

Fractured Fractions

This is a game for two players. The object of the game is to make two fractions and find their sum. Whoever has the greater sum is the winner.

Use index cards or regular playing cards to make two sets of the numbers 1 through 6. If using playing cards, have the aces represent the 1's.

Shuffle the cards, and place them facedown. Player one draws the top three cards and chooses two to write a proper fraction on his or her sheet. Then player two repeats the process. This continues until both players have each drawn six cards and written two proper fractions on their game sheets. Both players should then find the sum of both fractions. If they disagree about the sum, they should work the problems together until they agree on the correct answer. The player with the greater sum is the winner. Be sure to change improper fractions to mixed numbers.

Player One Game Sheet　　　　　　**Player Two Game Sheet**

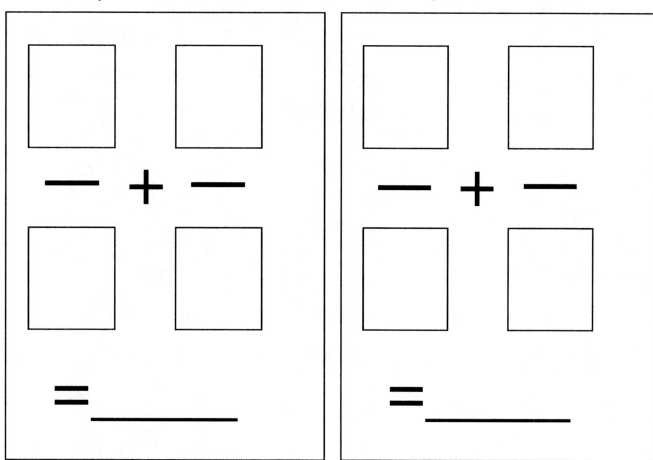

Game 33 ♫ ☺ ♫ ☺ ♫ ☺ ♫ ☺ ♫ ☺ ♫ ☺ ♫ ☺

Close the Box

This game is for two or more players. It requires the game board below, two dice, and nine counters such as beans, coins, small disks, etc. The object of the game is to have the lowest score possible. The first player to reach 45 points is out.

To play the game, the first player rolls the dice. He or she can either cover both numbers shown or add them up and cover one number. For example, if a three and a four are rolled, the player can either cover the three and the four or just the seven. The same player continues rolling until he or she rolls a number that cannot be used. At that time, the remaining numbers are added up. If the sum is six or less, the player may discard one die and continue rolling the other one until he or she rolls a number that cannot be used. At that time, the sum of the remaining numbers is recorded as the player's score. If all of the numbers have been covered, the player earns 0 points. The board is then cleared, and it becomes the next player's turn. Play continues until there is only one player who has not reached 45 points. That player is the winner.

1	2	3
4	5	6
7	8	9

Game 34

Magic Squares

The numbers in a magic square add up to the same sum—up, across, or diagonally.

Use the numbers listed below to place in the boxes so that each column, each row, and each of the two diagonals adds up to the stated number for that magic square.

Magic Square One—Use the numbers 3, 4, and 5 to fill the squares so that each column, each row, and each of the two diagonals adds up to 12. Each number must be used three times.

Magic Square Two—Use the numbers 10, 11, and 12 three times each so that each column, each row, and each of the two diagonals adds up to a total of 33.

Magic Square Three—Use the numbers 1 and 2 eight times each so that each column, row, and diagonal adds up to 6.

Magic Square One

Magic Square Two

Magic Square Three

Game 35 ⟳ ⟲ ⟳ ⟲ ⟳ ⟲ ⟳ ⟲ ⟳ ⟳ ⟳ ⟲ ⟳ ⟲

I've Been Framed!

Each number in the large boxes below is written within a smaller different shape or frame. Using this as a guide, write the correct number in each shape below and solve each problem.

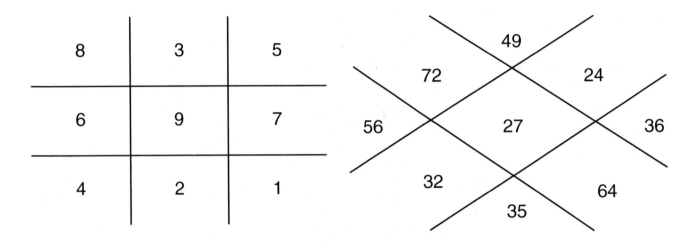

1. $(\wedge \div \llcorner) \times (\diamondsuit \div \sqcup) = $ _____

2. $(\diagup\rangle \div \urcorner) \times (\vee \div \sqsubset) = $ _____

3. $(\diagdown\rangle \div \square) \times (\langle\diagup \div \lrcorner) = $ _____

4. $(\rangle \div \sqsubset) \times (\sqcap\diagdown \div \lrcorner) = $ _____

5. $(\langle \div \sqsupset) \times (\wedge \div \sqsubset) = $ _____

Game 36 ✺ ✺ ✺ ✺ ✺ ✺ ✺ ✺ ✺ ✺ ✺ ✺ ✺ ✺ ✺

Division Mix-Up

The top boxes contain division problems, and the bottom ones contain the answers. Work each problem and find its answer in the bottom boxes. Then, write the word from the problem box into the correct answer box. Your result will be a funny saying!

Problems

926 ÷ 4 **a**	473 ÷ 6 **optometrist**	416 ÷ 9 **made**	493 ÷ 7 **and**
1,729 ÷ 8 **of**	3,414 ÷ 5 **herself**	4,121 ÷ 3 **into**	3,210 ÷ 4 **fell**
2,057 ÷ 3 **lens grinder**	3,002 ÷ 6 **The**	2,751 ÷ 8 **spectacle**	5,605 ÷ 7 **the**

Answers

500 (r2)	78 (r5)	802 (r2)	1373 (r2)
800 (r5)	685 (r2)	70 (r3)	46 (r2)
231 (r2)	343 (r7)	216 (r1)	682 (r4)

Game 37

Improper Fraction Mix-Up

The top boxes contain improper fractions, and the bottom ones contain mixed numbers. For each improper fraction, find its mixed number in the bottom boxes. Then write the word from the improper fraction box into the correct mixed number box. Your result will be a funny saying!

3/2 never	7/4 loved	10/8 It	16/12 person	11/7 have	15/9 a
16/10 loved	19/11 than	24/10 better	14/12 to	22/13 is	21/15 to
13/9 lost	16/14 short	22/18 have	18/10 tall	33/24 and	33/18 a
1 1/4	1 9/13	2 2/5	1 2/5	1 4/7	1 3/5
1 3/8	1 4/9	1 2/3	1 1/7	1 1/3	1 8/11
1 1/2	1 1/6	1 2/9	1 3/4	1 5/6	1 4/5

Game 38

Parting Advice

Some parting advice is hidden below. To find it, follow these directions. Find the fraction of the word in each problem below. As you find each fraction, write the letters in order into the boxes at the bottom of the page. The first one has been started for you.

1. the first $\frac{1}{2}$ of love

2. the second $\frac{1}{2}$ of book

3. the first $\frac{2}{3}$ of ink

4. the first $\frac{1}{3}$ of ate

5. the first $\frac{3}{5}$ of mirth

6. the last $\frac{1}{2}$ of horror

7. the first $\frac{3}{5}$ of where

8. the last $\frac{1}{3}$ of hen

9. the first $\frac{6}{7}$ of combine

10. the first $\frac{1}{2}$ of go

11. the first $\frac{3}{5}$ of young

12. the last $\frac{1}{3}$ of car

13. the first $\frac{2}{3}$ of hat

14. the last $\frac{2}{5}$ of chair

| L | O | | | | | | | |

Game 39 ꙩ ꙮ ꙩ ꙮ ꙩ ꙮ ꙩ ꙮ ꙩ ꙮ ꙩ ꙮ ꙩ ꙮ

Astounding Rounding

Follow the directions to discover a hidden message! Round the numbers below and find the answer in the answer column. The number in front of the answer tells you where to put each letter that you will find in front of the number to be rounded.

M	71,845 to the nearest ten	1. 459,060
C	459,056 to the nearest hundred	2. 71,850
S	459,056 to the nearest ten	3. 6,572,650
A	6,572,653 to the nearest million	4. 72,000
F	6,572,653 to the nearest hundred thousand	5. 459,000
L	71,845 to the nearest thousand	6. 6,573,000
I	6,572,653 to the nearest ten	7. 71,800
Y	6,572,653 to the nearest ten thousand	8. 459,050
U	459,056 to the nearest hundred thousand	9. 6,572,700
E	459,056 to the nearest thousand	10. 70,000
V	459,056 to the nearest ten thousand	11. 460,000
O	71,845 to the nearest ten thousand	12. 6,570,000
R	6,572,653 to the nearest hundred	13. 500,000
T	6,572,653 to the nearest thousand	14. 6,600,000
W	71,845 to the nearest hundred	15. 7,000,000
P	459,046 to the nearest ten	16. 459,100

$$\overline{}\ \overline{}\ \overline{}\ \overline{}\ \overline{}\quad \overline{}\ \overline{}\qquad \overline{}\ \overline{}\ \overline{}\ \overline{}$$
$$\ \ 1\quad 2\quad 3\quad 4\quad 5\qquad 3\quad 6\qquad\ \ 7\quad 3\quad 4\quad 4$$

$$\overline{}\ \overline{}\ \overline{}\ \overline{}\ \overline{}\ \overline{}\ \overline{}$$
$$\ \ 3\quad 2\quad 8\quad 9\quad 10\quad 11\quad 5$$

$$\overline{}\ \overline{}\ \overline{}\ \overline{}\quad \overline{}\ \overline{}\ \overline{}\ \overline{}$$
$$\ 12\quad 10\quad 13\quad 9\qquad 14\quad 15\quad 16\quad 5$$

$$\overline{}\ \overline{}\ \overline{}\ \overline{}\ \overline{}$$
$$\ 11\quad 15\quad 4\quad 13\quad 5$$

Answer Key

Page 4

1. $9 - 8 + 6 + 3 - 5 + 1 = 6$
2. $5 - 3 + 4 + 4 - 2 + 9 = 17$
3. $5 + 3 + 2 - 4 + 1 - 5 = 2$
4. $3 + 2 - 1 + 4 + 1 - 3 = 6$
5. $5 - 1 - 1 + 3 + 4 + 8 = 18$
6. $4 + 9 - 3 + 7 + 3 - 1 = 19$
7. $2 - 1 + 8 + 9 - 3 + 5 = 20$
8. $8 + 7 + 1 - 4 - 4 + 6 = 14$
9. $7 - 6 + 2 + 9 - 9 - 3 = 0$
10. $3 + 5 - 3 + 9 + 6 - 5 = 15$

Page 5

1. 35001; loose
2. 38076; globe
3. 5338; bees
4. 710; oil
5. 3504; hose
6. 771; ill
7. 0.04008; boohoo
8. 7718; Bill
9. 35108; Boise
10. 618; big

Page 6

1. 771; ill
2. 7735; sell
3. 35001; loose
4. 710; oil
5. 0.7734; hello
6. 0.02; zoo
7. 376616; giggle
8. 3045; shoe
9. 808; Bob
10. 0.40404; hohoho
11. 3704; hole
12. 7105; soil
13. 638; beg
14. 505; SOS
15. .09; go

Page 7

Answers will vary.

Page 9

Answers will vary.

Page 10

For metric answers convert the following U. S. Customary responses accordingly.

A1. 7,000,000,000

A2. the population of the United States

A3. an almanac

A4. Divide the number of cookies by the population figures.

B1. 90 million over 150 million; three-fifths

B2. 50 million; find out what fraction 30 million is of 90 million (one-third) and the one-third of 150 million to 50 million.

C1. Divide 150 million pounds by 10 to 15 million pounds.

C2. One solution: You already know that 150 million cookies equals 10 times around the globe. Fifteen times is half again as much as ten so divide 150 million by 2. Add that figure to 150 million. The equation will read 150 million + 75 million = 225 million.

D1. Multiply 33,000 by 7, which is the number of days in a week, to get 231,000.

D2. Divide 33,000 by 24 to get 1,375.

Page 11

1. motion
2. kinetic
3. Wind
4. energy
5. Heat
6. Sound
7. Electricity
8. changed

Page 14

1. 258
2. 774
3. (39) 813
4. (81) 732
5. 1,464
6. 13,176
7. (4) 3,294
8. (513) 2,781
9. (1,290) 1,491
10. (380) 1,871 – 9 = 1,862

Page 16

Fractions: 2/4, 3/6; 1/3; 2 2/3; 8 1/6; 1 3/8

Measurements: 12; 18; 1; Fahrenheit, Celsius; area = 1/2 bh

Word Problems: 28; 105; $399.00; roller blade time; how many bags she picked

Time: quarter till three; 180; 4; 100; 4 hrs. 5 min.

Page 18

1. 21	8. 18	15. 32
2. 7	9. 69	16. 8
3. 9	10. 92	17. 3
4. 2	11. 36	18. 8
5. 8	12. 25	19. 20
6. 7	13. 53	20. 85
7. 5	14. 91	

Page 21

Elsie	Elsie	giggles
leg	egg	Lee
hill	Lee	Elsie
Lee	Elsie	gosh
hi	gobble	shell
Lee		

Page 23

Page 24

1. 15
2. 38
3. 44
4. 69
5. 75
6. 91
7. 99
8. 95
9. 117
10. 141
11. CDIX
12. MCXV
13. MDCLXI
14. MDCCL
15. MCMXL
16. XII
17. XIV
18. XXIX
19. MDCCCXXIV
20. MCMXLIX

Page 25

1. 27,880
2. 37,267
3. 71,503
4. 671,605
5. 754,279
6. 39,658
7. 621,678
8. $11,108
9. 673,801; 8,912

Pages 26 and 27

1. 8 ft.
2. 34 cm
3. 961 cm^2
4. 9 m
5. 12 in., 12 in.
6. 102 ft.
7. 7 m
8. 162 ft.^{2}

Page 30

1. 6	6. 4
2. 7	7. 16
3. 5	8. 18
4. 3	9. 15
5. 6	10. 4

Page 31

Steal Its Chair

Page 32

1. 57—3
2. 310—2, 5, 10
3. 108—2, 3, 4, 9
4. 4,325—5
5. 232—2, 4
6. 135—3, 5, 9
7. 3,870—2, 3, 5, 9, 10
8. 3,720—2, 3, 4, 5, 10
9. 18,411—3
10. 891—3, 9

Page 33

1. 8 in.	5. 343 in.^{3}
2. 7 cm	6. 5 cm
3. 1,210 cm^3	7. 1,000 in.^{3}
4. 2 in.	8. 2 cm

Page 36

2, 3, 5, 7, 11, 13, 17, 19, 23, 29, 31, 37, 41, 43, 47, 53, 59, 61, 67, 71, 73, 79, 83, 89, 97

Page 41

1. 3, 5, 4, 5, 4, 3, 4, 3, 5
2. 10, 12, 11, 12, 11, 10, 11, 10, 12
3. 1, 2, 2, 1, 2, 1, 1, 2, 1, 2, 2, 1, 2, 1, 1, 2

This is one possibility. Accept other correct responses.

Page 42

1. $(35 \div 5) \times (27 \div 3) = 63$
2. $(32 \div 4) \times (49 \div 7) = 56$
3. $(72 \div 9) \times (24 \div 8) = 24$
4. $(56 \div 7) \times (64 \div 8) = 64$
5. $(36 \div 6) \times (35 \div 7) = 30$

Page 43

The optometrist fell into the lens grinder and made a spectacle of herself.

Page 44

It is better to have loved and lost a short person than never to have loved a tall.

Page 45

Parting Advice: Look in a mirror when combing your hair.

Page 46

Smile—It will improve your face value.